Fruit

Fruit

A Collection

By Jade Finnigan

Copyright © 2020 by Jade Finnigan

All rights reserved. No part of this book may be used or reproduced in any manner whatsoever without written permission except in the case of reprints in the context of reviews.

www.frillsandlyrics.com

ISBN-13: 9798681451044

Cover photography by Hannah Whitenstall

For Caitlin,

thank you for always trying to steal a glance at my notebook, for annotating my poems and for showing me when I'm deceiving myself.

Foreword

I want to say that this is entirely a work of fiction, but beneath any good fiction there is- of course- truth. Truth is not something that ought to be sacrificed in writing, so this is me trying to be truthful to the stories I know and the kinds of people I've encountered.

I've never wanted to force myself to write until the time was right. Until the words were fighting to come out. I've always said I'd wait to write the novel I've always dreamed of putting on the page, until I'd lived a bit more- after I'd gone out to make some memories and ended up with an enviable list of grave mistakes. Now, although I've been locked up indoors for nearly 6 months, I still feel like I have finally found something I feel I have to say in this form, even if it is just a little. An unrestrained reflection in celebration of the follies of my adolescence and the relationships that define it.

2020 has undoubtedly been a difficult year for most, regardless of how that struggle manifested for each individual. I don't want to write it off or delete it from my memory though, because I have been fortunate enough to have gained clarity as a result of that difficulty.

Fruit, for me, is a love letter to the wishful thinking that can plague us all. The moments where you dream of something you do not need. The moments where you fail to see the mess collecting at your feet. Even the ones where you're cruel out of envy, or ignorant out of hope. As well as, the times where you wish you were someone you're not. *Someone that you'll never be.* As damaging as those moments may be, they're fundamental to this human experience and that's what comes across as most beautiful to me- the primitive, the indelible and the fleeting.

With hindsight, I've come to realise that not enough is gained from exhausting yourself trying to maintain *the person you put on in the morning*, to make it worthwhile. Save your energy. Be the person who you need yourself to be. And I know, it's easier said than done- I've probably failed more days than I've succeeded, but having the intention to live for yourself and not succumb to the pressure of a persona, is what I find to be the best thing you can do. After all, perfect doesn't exist, and if it did, it would be ugly.

But then again, who am I to tell you what to do? I'm only on the verge of eighteen, have been known to squeal when I stall the car as the lights go green, and the boys that make me cry smell of Lynx Africa yet still manage to invade my dreams.

I hope this collection helps you appreciate or reminds of you of a time when you were as foolish as me.

Jade

Contents

Flower Bed 1

eschatology 2

'In the mornings' 3

Imitation Game 4

'We grow into our names' 5

Disengaged 6

Our little girl 7

'I allow myself to feel the cold' 8

'In January, I'm brave' 9

A folly of youth 10

'What is love?' 11

'It's not that I don't wish' 12

Fruit 13

Fate 14

staring at the ceiling 15

Scalpel 16

Reconciliation 17

Me in a different font 18

Fight me. 19

Your favourite song 20

solace 21

Amber 22

Scab 23

Flower Bed

All the colour this town can offer me
can be summarised to that of the second flower bed on St Faith's.
It thrived outside of the shadow of the empty museum
and was where we sat that day
because we're an indecisive pair
and me, trying too hard not to care,
suggested we clamber in amongst the blooms
to enjoy the August light.

I laughed way too hard as you spoke -
'til I'd cried mascara down my face
and I couldn't tell you what for, because
I don't remember a word that was said.
But what I do remember is
every colour in that bricked off plot:
from the purpling sweet peas
to the blazing dahlias
or the reflection of the sky in your eyes.

Every time I look at you, think of you,
or even say your name,
I cannot help but see every colour,
and they spin into this bright white light around you,
so you glow
even as you sit in a flower bed, fiddling with twigs.

eschatology

you, me and a bottle of rum

waiting for the hypersonic missiles to come

lying back into your arms

watching our dreams burn like stars

clinging to each other's hands

as we lie there on the white sand

stay silent as the sun descends -

that's how we were meant to watch the world end

In the mornings

I pull back my hair

Take out my contacts

Push nails through my ears

Cling film my complexion

Take out my hot glue gun

and press my lips shut.

Imitation Game

I'm trying to reflect back at you what you deserve to see-

To be the picture-perfect response

Worthy of the silver screen.

I don't deny my flaws,

So that you still trust me.

But I want to be your salvation,

muse and inspiration.

We grow into our names.

Choose wisely

For, what they call us is what we will become.

Disengaged

Night falls and finally, I can admire all that's above
with no risk of going blind.
I look up though and I'm deluged with vertigo, because
I can't see the stars -

Above me, flits a blazing flag
dancing to the wind.
It's just the one, but
then there's two and soon
I'm struggling to make out any blue,

So I clamber up the flagpole and
paint each one stark white.

I soon exhaust myself with the same vain ritual and
instead, confine my gaze to the road ahead because
eventually the rain will come and
the storm will tear them down, so
I am left
scrambling through sodden swathes of crimson
trying not to drown

Our little girl

To the girl in the cornflower dress,

with uncut blonde hair

and thighs still the width of ankles,

I hope you don't become enamoured by the mirror,

for she doesn't spring eternal.

I allow myself to feel the cold

I love the way it dents my bones

and hollows my capillaries

Romanticise the downpour, my love

for though this is Britain,

cynicism does not require submission

In January, I'm brave -

Manifest a change

But I sleep under duvets in July,

And wear turtlenecks in November.

A folly of youth

You keep promising me you're awake, but I can see your eyes shutting.

A nod and vague mumble are not going to convince me otherwise.

I keep talking at your sleepy face on the screen regardless,

but keep the blanket over my head

and my volume to a whisper because

it's long past midnight

and my parents don't know I'm awake.

The first time you fell asleep,

I called you back,

so the ringing would wake you up,

but you told me not to do that again

because your parents will catch us.

So, the next time you fall asleep,

I just look at you.

Your phone's propped up against a lamp

that's veiling your face in golden light

and you look at peace;

finally vulnerable.

I know you're probably dreaming of me,

so I utter 'I love you' and pray to God

- I hope it's true.

What is love?

Well, I know it's not us

keeping canned fruit in the freezer.

It's not that I don't wish you

could mean more to me,

you just cannot be what I think I *need*

- my lust is for a fantasy.

Fruit

The skin gathers and wrinkles

under the pressure of her thumbs- prying it open

from the pedicel mound.

Bursting.

And through the gaps between her fingers

Its sticky sangria syrup

runs down the gutters of her hand

into the cuff of her sleeve

Fate

I sit by my spindle

Endlessly churning out red yarn.

My fingers bleed and blister,

But it's fair because

I damn each human with

'the one'.

staring at the ceiling

sometimes

I wish I'd written poems

in those days

when I'd stare at the ceiling for hours

thinking about you

rather than now

when I'm bitter and broken

Scalpel

I would study for fourteen years, if that is what it takes-

spend all I've got on textbooks and never miss an A.

I'd take placements, so I could observe

the masters at their work.

And during each dissection, I'd tape my eyelids open

- though I cower at spilt blood -

so I could cut you like a surgeon

and disguise the fact that I'm a lumberjack in scrubs.

Reconciliation

She blotted her lipstick;

pruned her grandiose head of curls;

then put on barely a dress

- thin and blue and marked with white blossom.

She then smothers her figure

with her dad's old jumper;

and is sure to pull down the hem,

before retracting her hands

into the sullied cuffs

- where she's safe.

She lifts her chin,

and goes to see

him

Me in a different font

I'd call her 'btec',

but I'm politically correct,

and a feminist

who rather pities her.

Though, you'll only ever love

the idea

because that's what you did

to me.

I like to think that when you fuck,

you see my face

cuz we both know that she's just me,

in a different font.

Fight me.

we never fought

come to think of it

never really had anything

to say

about anything

that we didn't agree on

which wasn't much

we'd go round

in empty circles

with smiles stamped

on our face

I was not made to be that way

but that's what you get

for being in it for the sex

Your favourite song

Do you regret playing me your favourite song?

Giving it away?

Well, you shouldn't.

Though it may make you ache

and you'll never listen to it the same,

I still hear it

then the thought of you burdens me all day,

so now it belongs to you more than ever,

more so than it ever did to the writer

because it's your legacy,

indelibly burnt into me.

Now, isn't that just glorious?

solace

there's a place I go

to make me feel small

to get out of my head

and remind me of the

impermanence of it all

it's a place where the horizon's uninhibited

and red clay tiles stretch

as far as the eye can see

i can make myself fit inside a square metre

whilst billions of other stories surround me

i'm fragile enough for a gust of wind to deter

and nothing else alleviates

like allowing yourself to

Stop trying.

Amber

I want to thank you,

I'm not entirely sure what for,

But perhaps it's the way you can read my mind,

The way you drown out my thoughts,

Bring me to that moment of quiet

Before the suffocation sets in.

Maybe it's the way you soothe my demons

By confronting them face on.

You pick me apart

As you hold me

together.

We're a glue that doesn't quite set.

I want to thank you, Amber

For being my white noise.

Scab

Every bit of your debris -

I keep it in a box.

It is a little one.

We didn't last too long.

Cinema tickets

for a film we didn't see,

Bus tickets

for a side of town I'm not supposed to know,

Arcade tickets

that we coaxed out the machine,

and a photo.

I burned the negative a long time ago.

Once the contents of my wallet,

coat pocket, camera roll

lay covered in wait

for when it hurts no more.

Printed in Great Britain
by Amazon